Duplication

The Key to Creating Freedom in Your Network Marketing Business

Eric Lofholm
and
Judy O'Higgins

ERIC LOFHOLM INTERNATIONAL

Editorial direction by Roy Rasmussen
Interior design and layout by Marian Hartsough
Cover design by Marian Hartsough based on designs by Roy Rasmussen
    and Diego Rodriguez

Disclaimer: This book is intended to provide information only, and should not be construed as professional sales or business advice. No income claims are stated or implied. How you put this information to use is up to you.

ISBN-10: 0-9898942-2-3
ISBN-13: 978-0-9898942-2-7

Printed in the United States of America

Eric Lofholm
Eric Lofholm International
5701 Lonetree Blvd. Suite 121
Rocklin, CA 95765 United States
(916) 626-6820

Contents

Acknowledgments　　*vii*

Introduction by Eric Lofholm　　*ix*

Part I:
Duplication: The Key to Network Marketing Success　　1
(by Judy O'Higgins)

Chapter 1: The Duplication Concept　　3

Chapter 2: Three Keys to Duplicating Network Marketing Systems　　7
1. Have a System　　7
2. Keep Your System Simple　　8
3. Follow Your Simple System Consistently　　9

Chapter 3: Applying Duplication to Grow Distributors and Leaders　　11
1. Recruiting Distributors　　11
2. Training Distributors　　13
3. Training New Team Leaders　　14

Chapter 4: Duplication Takes Time　　17

Part II :
Duplicating Leadership (by Eric Lofholm)   19

Chapter 5: Duplicating Trainers: Repetition and the Training the Trainer Distinction   21

Chapter 6: Three Ways to Duplicate Network Leaders   25

1. Involve Your Leaders in Leading Meetings   26
2. Lead Training Events   27
3. Coach Three to Coach Three   28

Chapter 7: What Can Be Duplicated: Routine Procedures   31

Delegating Routine Tasks   31

Sharing Lists   31

Running One-on-one Meetings   32

Running Conference Calls   32

In-Home Party Hosting   32

Chapter 8: What Can't Be Duplicated: Respecting Individual Gifts and Talents   33

The Three-Foot Rule   33

Hotel Meetings   34

Natural Gifts   34

Conclusion: Duplicate the Success Formula   35

About the Authors   *37*

To Learn More   *38*

Dedication

*To the more than 65 million
network marketers around the world.*

Acknowledgments

Eric: I would like to acknowledge Tony Martinez, Tony Robbins, Michael Gerber, Dr. Donald Moine, and Ray Kroc for influencing my thinking on the concept of duplication.

Judy: I would like to acknowledge Eric for reminding me of my inner greatness and encouraging me to dream big and decide to go for my dreams.

Introduction by Eric Lofholm

This book reveals the biggest secret to network marketing success: ***duplication***. Duplication is essential to the concept of building a successful network marketing business. In contrast to other business models where success is measured by your personal success, if you want to succeed in network marketing, you've not only got to be personally successful: you've got to be able to duplicate your success in the people you recruit, and they've got to be able to duplicate it in others. This ability to duplicate your own efforts is what makes the network marketing business model so powerful. The task of duplicating yourself successfully is also what makes network marketing so challenging.

In order to duplicate yourself successfully, in order to not only teach your own recruits but also train them to teach others, you've got to know what's duplicable and what's not. For instance, you can teach anyone how to follow a checklist. You can teach anyone how to run an in-home party. You can teach anyone how to run a three-way phone call. Anyone can learn all these things because they're routine tasks that don't require any special skills.

But you can't teach things that depend on duplicating your personality or your personal aptitudes and skills. You can't teach an introvert to be an extrovert, which is the problem with teaching network marketing recruits to use the "three-foot rule". You can't teach someone who lacks charisma to run a weekly hotel meeting. You can't teach someone who hates technology to love to prospect on Facebook. In order to be able to duplicate your network marketing tactics with your recruits, you need a networking model that anyone can learn. That is what this book is designed to help you achieve.

I am excited to be writing this book with my coauthor Judy O'Higgins, who I often talk about on my training calls because I'm so proud of her success. I asked Judy to write this book with me because I consider her to be one of the foremost network marketing experts and trainers in the world today! Judy has combined my strategies with her own network marketing genius to develop the brilliant strategies for duplicating downline success we'll be sharing in this book. Judy's strategies have propelled her to the top of her own company, where she currently leads a team of nearly 6,000 representatives in all 50 states and seven countries. As of the writing of this book Judy is ranked #16 out of 165,000+ reps in her company! Her strategies have proven themselves again and again in the way she's been able to help any company in any field in the network marketing industry duplicate her success. I consider Judy elite in the networking marketing industry, and would rank her in the top one-tenth of the top one-tenth of the top one percent of network marketing trainers in the world today.

My own perspective on network marketing has been shaped by learning firsthand from several of the top industry leaders over the past twenty years. Before I started my current career I was a cook at McDonald's, and although I didn't realize it at the time, later after I learned about network marketing I was able to reflect back on my experience and see the genius of Ray Kroc's duplication model at work in McDonald's phenomenal global success. I was also exposed to the idea of duplication by Michael Gerber, best-selling author of *The E-Myth*. I then became a trainer for Tony Robbins. While working for Tony we learned the same speaker model that Tony Robbins learned while working for the great Jim Rohn. So Tony duplicated himself in us trainers with great success. When I left Tony's organization to start my own training company, I was able to duplicate his success and grow my organization to over 10,000 students. About one-third of my clients are in network marketing or direct sales. In the course of my career I've helped thousands of clients apply my networking strategies to grow their own businesses.

Both Judy and I have a proven track record in network marketing, but this book isn't ultimately about her or about me. It's about how you can **duplicate** our success by applying the simple, proven strategies we're going to share with you in these pages. By learning and applying these strategies and sharing them with your downline team, your networking marketing business can have the same growth that Judy and I have enjoyed, and you can have the same leadership impact on your team as we've had on ours. We're going to give you a simple formula that works. Copying this successful model is the secret of **duplication**.

I'm going to let Judy talk for the next few chapters. Then at the end of the book I'm going to share some of my own applications of the duplication strategy she lays out here, and I'll also share an opportunity for you to learn more about how to duplicate our formula for network marketing success

Part I

Duplication: The Key to Network Marketing Success
(by Judy O'Higgins)

Chapter 1

The Duplication Concept

Mastering the duplication concept is the key to mastering network marketing because duplication is the engine that makes the business model of network marketing work. Essentially, duplication means that I can replicate a successful sale many times over through a team of other distributors in order to gather hundreds or thousands of customers instead of having to close each transaction myself. This is an example of using leverage to achieve massive results, and its brilliance lies at the heart of the network marketing business model.

To illustrate why duplication is such a powerful concept, imagine that you joined a network marketing company and they told you this: "In order to be successful, the first thing you are going to do is go out and find 300 people to purchase our product." That would sound very daunting to you, as it would to the 95 percent of us who are average, ordinary people and not sales superstars. Most of us would say "I can't do that" and quit before we even got started.

Now imagine the same network marketing company applying the concept of duplication. Imagine that instead of telling you that you had to find 300 people to purchase their product, they said "In order to be successful, the first thing you need to do is go out and find three people who will purchase our product and be your customers." Big difference! Anyone who loves the product and is willing to represent it can find three customers. This is a much more appealing, less intimidating goal for the average person.

Now let's take this to the next step. Imagine that your network marketing company then teaches you how to build a team of 10 other distributors like yourself using a system, and that each of the 10 distributors can find their three customers. That would produce a total of 30 customers buying your product on top of your own three personal customers—and you get paid a percentage of those 30 extra sales. The power of leverage is kicking in.

Next, each of your 10 team members learns how to duplicate what you have done, and builds their own team of 10 distributors each. Now you have a team of 100 total people. Each of them has followed the system and gathered three customers. You have acquired the 300 customers that your company asked you to do, but you only had to find three customers yourself! Then you trained 10 other distributors on your team to find three customers each, and taught them to duplicate that system. This is leverage at its best!

Because of duplication, success in network marketing isn't about you or me personally finding thousands of customers to use our companies' products and services. It's about you finding a few customers and finding a few other people who want to build a business with you, who each find a few customers and a few others who also want to build a business, and so on.

This is what makes network marketing such a perfect fit for the average person, the 95 percent of us from a wide variety of backgrounds who just want to create a better life for ourselves and our families. Being a sales superstar is not a requirement. You only need to be able to share your enthusiasm for your product to sign up a few customers. You also need to be able to share your business opportunity with others who are like-minded in order to build a team of other representatives doing the same. These are the only two things that we do to be successful in our profession.

Because of duplication, you don't need to be a sales superstar to be successful at network marketing; but what you DO need is an effective system for training your team to model what you do. The goal of duplication is for you to teach the other business builders on your team how to do what you have done so that eventually your business continues to grow without your direct effort, while you are getting paid a percentage of everyone's customer gathering and recruiting activity.

J. Paul Getty reportedly said "I would rather have 1% of the effort of 100 people than 100% of my own effort." The magic of network marketing is that it provides an unlimited number of opportunities to duplicate yourself and receive a share of the income generated by people you bring into your business.

By now you can see that learning how to teach others to duplicate what has worked for you is the key to massive growth and success in the network marketing business model. Therefore, as your team grows, the focus needs to be on using and teaching the best systems for recruiting, team building, and training. Helping others to duplicate the critical elements of your success is the name of the game for a winning team and a thriving business.

Chapter 2

Three Keys to Duplicating Network Marketing Systems

To successfully put the duplication concept into practice, there are three important keys you must implement. The first is having a system. The second is keeping your system simple. The third is following it consistently. Let me explain each of these key points.

1. Have a System

In order to duplicate a system, first you must have a system. I'm going to quote an old saying in network marketing here. "To have long-term success, network marketing involves a large group of people doing a few simple things over an extended period of time." Without a system to follow where everyone knows what the few simple things consist of, there's no duplication and massive growth won't happen.

Let's start with training a new team member. Every company has its own version of basic training for new distributors. This should be a critical starting place for teaching the two core activities of a successful network marketing business: how to gather customers and recruit other distributors. Most companies today have their own version of a fast-start plan that lays out very simple goals and actions for new distributors to accomplish in the first 30 days of their business. The fast-start plan typically has built-in financial incentives to encourage the new distributor to take action right away instead of waiting days or weeks until they think that they know enough to get started. The financial incentives create urgency so that the new team member will be motivated to get started right away in order to earn their first paycheck.

This fast-start plan is a blueprint, and it is where duplication begins. Every new person gets started the same way with the same track to run on for their first 30 days. If everyone just completed the fast-start 30-day program and helped their first few recruits to do the same, duplication would happen automatically.

Human nature being what it is, some people will follow direction and complete their 30-day fast-start plan, and some won't. However, the system is clearly there for those who choose to get started right and it works.

2. Keep Your System Simple

Next let's talk about simplicity. For a fast-start system to be effective, it must first and foremost be simple. Computers and technology may work well with complexity, but human beings do best with simplicity in order to duplicate what another has done. For duplication to happen, anyone of any age, background or educational level must be able to follow the system. It must work for them as it did for those who came before them. It must also work for anyone in their downline who follows it exactly.

Why is having a very simple fast-start training system in place so important? Because most people starting into a new network marketing business have no idea what to do or how to get started! They desperately need a simple step-by-step guide to show them what actions to take along with a deadline to complete them in order to receive a reward. With this tool, the obstacle is overcome and the idea that you have to be some kind of marketing superstar to succeed is vanquished.

If the 30-day plan is simple and clear, the new person will believe that they can actually do it. In fact, belief is arguably the most critical element because it doesn't matter how great the company's basic training plan is: if the new person doesn't believe they can accomplish it, then they are never really going to even try, and it's already all over for them.

A perfect example of always keeping training simple is the person who personally sponsored me in my network marketing company. He has taught the same simple ideas and action steps for almost 10 years and has gone straight to the top of our company by creating the largest team. Because he follows the KISS principle consistently (Keep it Simple Stupid), everyone on his team believes that they can do what he teaches and they take action. He has been our #1 money earner from the year he got started, and keeping it simple is his secret.

3. Follow Your Simple System Consistently

The third key is following your system consistently. For duplication to happen, the simple system that your company and your team leaders teach must be followed consistently, not just some of the time. This is because it's the system that's the big deal, not the personality or talent of any one distributor. Neither personality nor talent is duplicable. The system is.

You can't base a successful system on duplicating personality. Some distributors aspire to be the center of attention and build a team based on everyone bowing down to them as the guru, the one who makes everyone else successful by doing all the presentations, closing everyone's prospects, and running all the team trainings. This is actually a recipe for disaster, even though it may be great for the leader's ego and it may seem attractive on the surface.

First of all, the guru is going to burn themselves out from doing all these activities themselves instead of teaching others how to do them independently. Think of the guy in the variety show who's spinning plates on a stick. When a plate starts to wobble and fall, he runs over and gets it restarted. Meanwhile, on the other end of the stage, two more plates start to wobble and fall, and then he starts to run quickly over to them only to see that more are wobbling and falling faster than he can run to fix them.

This perpetual plate-spinning race is the life of a network marketing guru who thinks he is the only one who can make everything work. He ends up burned out and quitting the business. Meanwhile, his team has not learned to be independent and follow a system. They just let him do it all. Because he convinced them he was the best one to do it, they have not learned to do the presentations, how to recruit team members on their own, or how to run team trainings. So when he's gone, they're crippled in their business by not knowing how to duplicate its success.

The moral of the story is: follow the system, not the guru!

Another trap to be wary of is the person who wants to reinvent the wheel and create a new system, a better mousetrap. This type of person may go off on a tangent and take their team with them, only to find that each time they do this, it takes a long time for others to learn their new and improved system and business growth is slowed down accordingly.

In network marketing, reinventing the wheel is usually not a good idea. Some people on the team will follow the leader's new ideas, while others will stick with the company's proven plan. Soon everybody's doing something different, which is not conducive to duplication. Duplication is based on:

1. Having one system

2. Keeping it simple

3. Everyone on the team following it consistently

For a team that is equipped with an effective and simple fast-start system, the possibilities for growth are endless.

Chapter 3

Applying Duplication to Grow Distributors and Leaders

The next thing I want to share is some specific places where applying duplication to the network marketing process is most vital. There are three key applications: recruiting distributors, training distributors, and training team leaders.

1. Recruiting Distributors

Let's start with recruiting. I've identified three key places in the recruiting process where it's very important that everybody be saying or doing the same thing.

The Interest-Creating Remark

The first place is when you're speaking to someone in the very beginning stages about your business. What you're doing at that point is basically creating curiosity in the prospect. Eric calls this using an interest-creating remark (ICR).

Here's an example of an interest-creating remark that we're teaching everyone in my company to say now that's so simple it's ridiculous: "If I could show you a way to get paid for simply being nice to people, would you want to find out about it?" Now, anyone can say that. It creates curiosity, it's simple, and it's very easily taught.

Using Your Company Tools

Here's another example. Let's say the person that you are speaking to is curious and wants to know more. At that point, instead of you explaining everything and becoming the center of the presentation yourself, it's very important to use a tool that the company gives you. In my company, after I say the interest-creating remark, if they're interested, then I give them a DVD to watch. That's what the company teaches everyone to do. It's the same DVD for everybody.

If you don't have a DVD handy or you're talking over the phone, you point the person to your self-replicating website that everyone in the company has. Each representative's site has the exact same video prominently displayed. All the visitor has to do is push play. You refer prospects to the website and make an appointment for following up. So basically, you're not doing the presentation: you're using technology tools to do it for you, and everyone's using the same tools.

Follow-up Questions

The third key place to apply duplication to recruiting is when you're in the follow-up stage. At this point you want to ask the person you're recruiting a question. We're teaching everyone to ask the same question to start out with. The question is: "What did you like best about what you just saw?" Pretty simple and very duplicable.

We are also teaching our team members to "close" with the "1 to 10 Scale" question. It sounds like this: "May I ask you a question, Mr. Prospect? On a scale of 1 to 10 with 1 being 'I have no interest at all in your company and you are wasting my time' and 10 being 'I really like this and I am ready to get started now,' where do you see yourself?" This is followed by, "What would it take for you to be a 10?" With everyone using the same closing questions, it becomes easy to help both old and new distributors overcome their fear of not knowing what to say at the end of the follow-up process to "close" the prospect.

Those are three key areas of the recruiting process where duplication comes in. It's a simple system that anyone can learn. When distributors feel more confident from knowing how to speak with a prospect using a simple interest creating remark, how to present to that prospect using a tool instead of having to do all the talking, and what to say when following up, then they are more likely to take more action, talk to more people, and have more recruiting success.

2. Training Distributors

Let's move on to training. The person you shared your business opportunity with signed up and became a new distributor on your team, and now they need to be trained. I have identified four areas where using a system can create or enhance duplication in the training process.

The Checklist

Each new distributor should immediately get a checklist of things to do right away.

It needs to be the same checklist for every new person. It should be updated on a consistent basis and shared with all members of the team to use with their new recruits. If everyone uses this system, new representatives will be less likely to fall through the cracks or go off on their own tangent, and everyone starts off on the same foot.

The Fast-start Program

Next is the fast-start program previously discussed that is created by most companies as an action plan for brand new distributors in order to earn their first check. If your company has created training tools for this fast-start plan such as a video or a printed brochure, make sure that everyone uses them the same way to train their new person, giving all new distributors an equal chance to get off to a good start in their new business. The trainer or sponsor needs to thoroughly explain every step to the new recruit, either in person or by phone and actively help them to set and achieve their first goals.

Ongoing Training

Every company has an ongoing training program for everyone in the entire distributor base. This is normally done by corporate trainers and/or by the top distributor field leaders on a weekly basis, using technology to reach the masses in the field. This could consist of webinars, conference calls, video conferencing, or all of the above. The important thing is to make sure every (new and old) distributor knows about these regular trainings and is aware of the importance of building these events into their weekly schedules. If everyone listens in or watches, then training information, new promotions, and company announcements reach every single person on the team immediately. Make it part of your company and team culture that everyone gets on these calls and receives the same information simultaneously or listens to the replays right away. This will speed up duplication by eliminating the need to explain the information contained in the calls over and over to people who were not there. Again, everyone is on the same page by following a system.

Live Events

Similar to the ongoing training just described, every company puts on live events for their distributors in order to build belief, create a sense of community, and provide live training opportunities. Just as with the conference calls and webinars, it is vital for all distributors to attend these events—perhaps even more so, because they not only impart information but spark motivation in the field to go home and take more action.

In fact, to create more duplication on your team, it can be argued that getting your distributors to attend live events is the single most important thing you can do to grow your team, because of these multiple benefits. This is especially true for the annual company convention, where many people that were thinking of quitting their network marketing business have been totally re-energized, returning home and totally turning their business around and then going on to great success! Make it a given in your team culture that going to events is expected, and watch your team duplicate faster!

3. Training New Team Leaders

The last area is training new team leaders. This comes into play after the distributor has followed your lead and duplicated you and they've built a small team of their own. They're on their way and maybe they've achieved their first company promotion. At this point you groom the distributor for an emerging role in leading their growing team.

The first key to achieving this is have them start running their own home meetings. It's a very good idea to have a simple checklist of what the components of a successful home meeting are. Keep it simple and go over with them. Then help them to begin running their own home meetings and teaching their new distributors to do the same.

Second, have them practice sharing their two-minute success story and share it at small group meetings in your local area (for example at a restaurant or coffee shop) so they get used to being in front of a small group and sharing their story. Then perhaps have them work up to a larger role in that local group meeting.

Third, ask the person to begin to take leadership in assisting with the planning of special events or regional events. As previously described, all network marketing companies understand the power of events. Most of them want the local distributors to create regional events in cities around the country so that the leaders can use them as recruiting and training opportunities and as morale boosters to build momentum and excitement for the company.

Applying the same principle, if you do conference calls, start to give the emerging leaders some training roles on team conference calls. They can share their success stories or run parts of conference call training. When they're ready, you can ask them to do a whole business opportunity or group training for a larger group.

As your team expands all over the country, you'll make more use of conference calls and webinars. To sustain duplication throughout this growth, I recommend having regular conference calls with your established team leaders. These calls are the time to go over things like the new distributor checklist and the procedures for all the different things that I just mentioned. Make sure that the leader in Seattle is teaching the same thing as the leader in North Carolina and the leader in Texas, so that everyone is teaching the same thing and everyone is all on the same page. This helps ensure that duplication is happening and that people are not going off on their own and reinventing the wheel.

Now you are duplicating leadership: the key to growing a massive and successful team.

Chapter 4

Duplication Takes Time

The final point I want to make goes back to the quote I referenced earlier that says, "Network marketing involves a large group of people doing a few simple things over an extended period of time." The part I want to emphasize here is the part that says "over an extended period of time." This is a mindset that needs to be understood, accepted, and passed on from the sponsor to each new distributor to head off unrealistic expectations that people often have when they start their new business. Network marketing, although it offers the opportunity to compress a 40-year career into a few years, still takes effort and time.

To succeed at network marketing, it's vital to develop the understanding early in the distributor training process that successful network marketing takes time. It is not a get-rich-quick business. It is not a quick fix for a major financial problem. To build up significant residual income (which is the income that comes in automatically month after month) normally takes three to five years and often longer to achieve true long-term financial freedom.

When new distributors understand this truth and come into their business with the right mindset and expectation that significant residual income is going to take time, they are much less likely to quit too soon before duplication has had a chance to occur in their business. They fully understand the importance of the element of time for duplication and team building to occur. This mindset will sustain them through the learning process and the early stages of their network marketing career so they can persevere long enough to enjoy the fruits of duplication in their business and have a real opportunity for long-term success.

At this time I am going to turn to Eric Lofholm to introduce his brilliance into the remaining chapters of this book. Eric has been one of my mentors for years and has amazing wisdom to share with you now.

Part II

Duplicating Leadership
(by Eric Lofholm)

Chapter 5

Duplicating Trainers: Repetition and the Training the Trainer Distinction

Now that Judy has shared some of her wisdom about how to apply duplication to network marketing, I'd like to share some of my own tips.

My perspective on duplication is a little bit different than Judy's because my background is different. Judy's perspective on duplication comes from her background of success in network marketing and counseling. Mine comes from sales training.

I was introduced to duplication working for McDonald's for three years. The McDonald's franchise is an ultimate example of duplication success. If you ever visit a McDonald's in another city, another state, or another country, you'll find that McDonald's are similar everywhere. McDonald's has a successful formula and their success stems from applying it consistently.

In reflecting on my experience at McDonald's, I became a subscriber to the mindset of Michael Gerber, best-selling author of *The E-Myth*. Gerber's fundamental concept was systematizing businesses by taking the McDonalds franchise model and applying it to your business even if you weren't planning on creating additional branches or franchising yourself. In other words, his approach was to systematize whatever processes you have even if it's just a single business.

Then I worked for Tony Robbins for three years. One key to Tony Robbins' success is that his company runs on systems. I was on a sales team when his organization was at its height. My team had six to eight of us at any one time. So Tony duplicated himself in each of us. We all went out, did what we were trained to do, and produced very, very predictable results. After leaving Tony's company Tony hired me back to train his sales team on the Jim Rohn Speaker Model. For two years I duplicated this model in about 50 people who went on to generate millions of dollars in revenue for Tony's company.

Then I started my own training company 15 years ago. My vision is to train and certify a million students in my system. To do this I've developed a system that develops the core set of ideas I want all my students to learn. I want all million of my students to be trained in the exact same fashion.

So just as in network marketing, there's a duplication component in my business where I'm teaching everybody the same methodology, the same process, the same system. On the basis of that experience, I've developed my own philosophies and ideas about duplication that fit well with what Judy teaches. That's why I wanted to team up with Judy and get her network marketing perspective and combine it with my perspective from my business experience.

One of my key duplication philosophies is repetition. Repetition is where you do the same thing over and over and over again. So you do the three-way call the same way every time. You do the in-home meeting, you do the hotel meeting, you do the top 25 list or the top 200 list the same way every time. The purpose of that repetition, doing it over and over and over again, is that it produces predictable results.

So I am somebody who really likes predictability in my business, and when I train somebody, I like them to get the same predictable results that I'm getting. That's why my approach to duplication emphasizes the concept of systems that produce predictable results.

One of the systems that I'm a firm believer in is a distinction I call "Train the Trainer." In my business that means that we learn by teaching. I teach that there are different ways to learn. One way to learn is intellectually. The second way to learn is experientially, by doing. Then the third way to learn is by teaching others.

As you're reading the book, you're learning from Judy and myself. To apply the Train the Trainer distinction, as you're reading I want you to apply what you're learning by teaching others. Teach what you're reading to everybody on your team. When you go to your annual convention, when you're at your Super Saturday, when you're on your team weekly call, any time you're learning, you have two hats on. One hat is the hat to learn and apply what you're learning to yourself, while the other hat is to teach others. I teach my trainers to always be in that duplicable-oriented mindset of "I'm learning ideas to apply. I'm learning ideas to teach others."

My encouragement to you is to ingrain this mindset into the culture of your network marketing team so that everybody is thinking in terms of one, duplication and two, teaching others. What both Judy and I have experienced is that when we teach others, we actually get better ourselves. Teaching others is a systematic way for me to grow as a leader. My encouragement for all of you reading the book is that you make it the mindset of your network marketing culture that everybody on the team is a trainer: not just the people that have achieved rank, but everybody on the team. Everybody is a trainer.

Chapter 6

Three Ways to Duplicate Network Leaders

The key application of the Train the Trainer duplication distinction I want to teach you in this book is how to duplicate leadership development systems. There are different types of duplication. For instance, Judy discussed recruiting duplication when bringing on a new person. There are various aspects to duplication. What I'm going to focus on teaching you is how to apply duplication to leadership development systems.

The systems that I'm going to teach you here don't necessarily apply to everyone on your team. Some people on your team just want to come in and leverage the system the company has put together to drive people to webinars or in-home meetings, but they have no vision to do it themselves. This is fine because everybody isn't the same, as I'll discuss more later.

But you're going to have other people, people like you, that are the type of person who's inclined to get this book, read it, study it, and apply it. These people, like you, see themselves growing and becoming leaders in the organization. These are people you're going to be, in many cases, hand selecting and personally training and mentoring. The systems I'm teaching you here are designed to help you groom those people.

So it's a grooming system for leadership development. You're going to learn it, and then you're going to teach it to the people you groom. So if I bring in

Barbara and I'm grooming her to be a leader, I'm going to say, "Barbara, I want you to be selecting people that you're going to grab and groom them." The systems I'm discussing here are systems for developing people in whom you see potential for growing and becoming leaders in your organization. We need to wrap systems around these people so they can grow.

1. Involve Your Leaders in Leading Meetings

The first grooming system I want to share with you is involving the leaders you're grooming in leading business presentation meetings. These could be delivered as one-on-one coffee meetings, or over the phone, or through a conference call webinar, or at a hotel meeting, or at an in-home party. There are many different models for doing business presentations.

Whatever presentation model you use, as you're reading this, if you view yourself either already as a leader or as a future leader of your company, then you want to start delivering business presentations yourself. When you deliver the presentation yourself, every time you do it, you get a little bit better.

This is the power of a repetition. There's value in every rep. Even if you do a presentation and nobody signs up, it's still a rep under your belt. Every time you do it, you get a little bit better. This is why it's valuable to start doing presentations, or if you're already doing them, to increase the number of repetitions you're doing.

Then let's say you're now doing these presentations. The next step is to groom your future leaders to have them do part of the business presentation. My encouragement for you is not to ask them to volunteer to do it, but to tell them that they're actually doing it. In my experience in grooming people in my own business, if I wait for them to volunteer, they often don't take the initiative. However if I tell them they're doing it, they will more often do it.

So for example, I would go to Barbara on my team and I would say to her, "Barbara, I'm doing the business presentation on the webinar this Wednesday and one section is the company's story. Barbara, on this presentation, you're going to deliver the company's story." I would tell her that she's doing this, as opposed to asking her to do it. Now she's going to get butterflies, which is normal. But if she actually follows through and does it, she is going to grow a bit, and so is the company because a personnel resource nobody had every heard of before is now familiar to the rest of the team. This is a leadership development system.

The next step in this training system is having Barbara deliver a different section of the presentation. Gradually, I am grooming Barbara to lead the whole presentation herself.

So let's say it's a network marketing model where I'm doing it an-home party in my house every Wednesday night and Barbara comes to that meeting and she delivers her section of the presentation, and eventually she delivers the whole thing, I might encourage Barbara to branch off and have her own in-home parties. Maybe she does them on Tuesday nights or she does them a couple times a month, whatever the case may be.

But ultimately, I want to groom Barbara so she can branch off. Then I want to teach Barbara, "Okay, Barbara, you're now leading your own party in your house. You're going to look for people to groom within." That you're in the demo section of presentation that potentially, they are going to get the whole presentation, and then eventually, they're going to branch off and they're going to do it themselves, and then it's going to repeat.

So this is a very, very powerful way, a systematic way to duplicate yourself and grow leaders.

2. Lead Training Events

The next leadership development system I want to share involves training your team. You can train your team one-on-one. You can train them in weekly conference calls. You can train them on Super Saturdays. However you train your team, the concept that I want you, the reader of this book, to apply is to start leading trainings.

At first, you might just lead a section of the training event. For instance, you go to your team leader and say, "Hey, I have a topic I want to talk to the team about. Can I have ten minutes on the next conference call?" Hopefully they'll answer, "Okay, sure." When you do this, you might get some butterflies, but when you get that rep under your belt, and you do those ten minutes, you are going to get a little bit better. Then eventually, ultimately, I would love to see you leading your own trainings, your own Super Saturday, your own weekly call, your own one-on-one training sessions.

So let's say you're now leading your own team, and you and ten people on your team are plugging in weekly on Monday night, and you're doing this training. Next you're going to go to somebody in your team and say, "Hey, this week, we're working on building your list and I want you to do 10 minutes on building your list." They might say, "But I'm not even good at building my list. How am I going to train on that?" You reply, "That's exactly why I'm having you do it, because this is going to help you get better."

So you encourage Barbara to do ten minutes on building her list. Then Barbara can get butterflies, but those butterflies are actually a sign that she's growing. As she grows, eventually, she may lead her own training call perhaps, and she'll be grooming other people and duplicating your results.

This will create true leadership duplication in your business. This is something you want because as Judy was teaching earlier, you don't want to be the star, right? Of course you can be a star in your own right, but you want to really be the developer of stars. There's a distinction between a star and a star maker. The mindset for successful duplication is that you want to be a star maker. So you say to yourself, "Am I duplicating myself with my students? It's not really about me. It's about me duplicating myself in my students."

3. Coach Three to Coach Three

The third leadership development system I want to share is a distinction I call "Coach Three to Coach Three." The concept here is that leadership is transferred one-on-one. It's not transferred in the hotel ballroom.

An annual convention in a hotel ballroom is a wonderful thing. All successful network marketers always attend the annual convention. But from my viewpoint, that is not designed to develop leaders. It's designed for a lot of other benefits, but leadership is transferred in most cases one-to-one.

What I would encourage you to do is to select three people that you're grooming and personally coach them. That could look like a 30-minute one-on-one phone call each month. Or it could be a 1-hour phone call each month or two 30-minute calls. Or it could be you meet the person in a private meeting after a public business meeting.

Whatever model you use, the idea is that you're spending scheduled time on an ongoing basis with the people that you're grooming. Now, when I say "Coach Three to Coach Three," it could actually be Coach Five to Coach Five, it could be Coach One to Coach One. There's no magic in the number three, but Coach Three to Coach Three is just a simple way to explain it and teach you. You can adjust it to your needs, so that if you're training five leaders, then maybe for you it's Coach Five to Coach Five. Or if you have one leader that you're working on, it may be Coach One to Coach One.

But however you apply it, the concept is that you're spending one-on-one time coaching the people that you're grooming. The thing about it is that when you coach somebody else, you duplicate. You duplicate your knowledge in the person you're training, and you also duplicate your own success, because you yourself get better. The way you get better at coaching is you coach. Judy and I have both experienced this through many hours of one-on-one time with people in our various business ventures. Our blade is very sharp in our coaching because we've done so much one-on-one coaching. You can get really good at coaching, too, by practicing coaching.

So here's how you apply the concept. If I'm going to coach Barbara and groom Barbara, I'm going to say, "Hey, Barbara, I'm looking for three people to personally coach. Here's the deal: I'll coach you under this agreement and these conditions. Number One, you agree that you'll be active in the business. And you agree, Barbara that you will coach three as well. When the timing's right, you'll groom three other people. So you're active in the business. I'll groom you, I will one-on-one coach you, if you'll be active in the business and you agree to groom and coach three other people. Do you agree to do that?"

If Barbara says yes, then I'm going to coach her. Now, I'm not going to coach everybody. I'm just going to coach a couple. In this case, I'm just going to coach three people that I'm personally grooming. I'm going to add a scheduled time with Bob. It might be 30 minutes every other week, or it might be 1 hour once a week, whatever we agreed on. I'm going to budget some time commitment into my schedule to spend time with Bob coaching him. One of the ingredients to a successful relationship is time. I am just going to spend time and I'm going to pour my philosophies and my ideas into him.

And then Bob is going to do the same thing with others. Now, if I work with Bob and Mary and Steve, and then Bob, Mary, and Steve all agree to groom three, now we're going to impact the three people I'm coaching and the nine they're coaching. Now, we're duplicating leadership in twelve people.

Now, when Bob goes and grooms the three people he's training, he's going to say the same I said to him. So all Bob is going to say to Scott is, "Scott, here's the deal. I'll coach you and groom you. Number one, you got to be active in the business and Number Two, you have to be willing to groom three." Again, there's no magic in the number three. It could be five or it could be one, depending on what your goals are in your business model. The key point is that you're duplicating leaders by devoting one-on-one training time to transferring your skill set.

Chapter 7

What Can Be Duplicated: Routine Procedures

The last thing I want to share is about the concept of what's duplicable and what isn't. One problem network marketers run into is trying to duplicate things that aren't easily duplicable, so it's important to get this distinction. First let's start by identifying some things that are duplicable.

Delegating Routine Tasks

One thing you can duplicate is the effort you put into performing routine tasks. For instance, if you have a script for a call, you can delegate the task of making the call to someone else and save yourself time to perform other tasks such as training network leaders.

Sharing Lists

Another thing that's easy to duplicate is showing someone how to go through a top 25 list or a top 200 list. Anyone can read a list. Anyone can describe a list. Sharing lists is duplicable.

Running One-on-one Meetings

A third thing anyone can duplicate is running a one-on-one meeting. Anyone who can follow a routine procedure and work through a script can conduct a one-on-one meeting, whether they're doing it face-to-face or over the phone. Running a one-on-one meeting is duplicable.

Running Conference Calls

A fourth thing anyone can duplicate is running a three-way conference call. Running a three-way call is essentially similar to running a one-on-one call. You just have to learn to push a few extra buttons and make a few adjustments to the procedure and script in order to carry on an orderly conversation between all parties. Anyone who can run a one-on-one call can run a three-way call, and everyone can run a one-on-one call.

In-Home Party Hosting

A final thing that anyone can duplicate is an in-home party. We've all had guests over. Running an in-home party is just like having guests over while you follow a few additional items from your organization's checklist. Hosting in-home parties is easily duplicable by anybody.

What all of the above duplicable items have in common is that they are routine procedures following a sequence and script. Anyone can follow a set of procedures and a script if they're guided by a checklist and supported by materials such as brochures and videos. Anything that boils down to a sequence and a script is generally duplicable.

Chapter 8

What Can't Be Duplicated: Respecting Individual Gifts and Talents

I've been identifying some routine procedures that are duplicable because they follow a sequence and script. Now let me talk about what isn't so easily duplicable.

The Three-Foot Rule

Many network marketing organizations use the three-foot rule. The three-foot rule prescribes that you prospect anybody who gets within three feet of you. This is a great strategy for an extrovert.

However, the three-foot rule scares us introverts. In my natural style as an introvert, I am the kind of person that might sit on a plane and not talk to the person sitting next to me. My natural instinct is to put on my headphones and go off into my own world. So if you were my upline and you were telling me, "Eric, you've got to do this three-foot rule," I'd be thinking to myself, "I guess I can't do this business then." And most introverts will have the same natural reaction even if they don't necessarily tell you.

Now, by the way, the three-foot rule is a great strategy for the right person. It's just not an easily-duplicable strategy for an introvert. What Judy and I advocate is that instead of forcing the three-foot rule on a new recruit, you offer them a menu of eight to ten or so different tactics and invite them to select the ones that best fit their personal style. The three-foot rule can be one of these tactics. Others can include social media prospecting, networking, public speaking, webinars, phone calls, three-way calls, and teleconferences, for example. You may be able to suggest other tactics based on the person's unique qualities and activities. For instance, if you're recruiting a soccer mom who goes to all her children's games, it would be natural for them to use that as an opportunity to meet other parents.

Hotel Meetings

Another strategy that's not easily duplicable is a hotel meeting. To pull off a successful hotel meeting and offset the cost of the hotel, it requires a charismatic leader. Now in my case, even though I'm an introvert, I would be great for a hotel meeting because of my public speaking experience. But even though I would be great for a hotel meeting, if I recruit somebody who doesn't have the charisma, they probably won't be able to duplicate my results, and a hotel meeting led by them might end up being just an expense.

Natural Gifts

Another thing that's not duplicable is natural gifts. I call this a person's "energy advantage." Each person on your team has certain natural gifts which translate into their business strengths, and it's to your organization's advantage to promote their energy advantage. In other words, if they are great networkers, then encourage them to use their networking skills to build their network marketing business, even if the networking is not duplicable. If they're great at applying the three-foot rule, if they're great trainers, those are great assets in network marketing. But you lose this advantage if you try to force someone to focus on something they're not good at instead of encouraging them to develop their natural gifts.

What all of the above items have in common that makes them difficult to duplicate is that they rely on a person's personality. Being extroverted, charismatic, or naturally-gifted in a certain area reflects your personality. Each person is an individual, and you can't duplicate individuality. You can duplicate systems, but it still takes an individual to put those systems into effect, and you will get the most leverage from your systems if you respect the natural personalities, gifts, and talents of the individuals who make up your organization instead of expecting them to duplicate your leader's personality.

Conclusion

Duplicate the Success Formula

In this book Judy and I have shared a proven formula for network marketing success. The duplication formula has worked for me for 18 years since I first started applying it under Tony Robbins. It's worked for Judy for nine years in network marketing. It works for Judy's 6,000 representatives. It will work for you if you put what you've read here into action.

But taking action is one of those other things that isn't duplicable. Taking action is something everyone has to do for themselves. I invite you to take action on the ideas Judy and I have shared in this book. I encourage you to make a commitment to applying what you've learned.

Put Judy's strategies into action. Make sure you have a system, make sure it's simple, and make sure you and your team are following it consistently. Follow Judy's steps for training distributors and leaders.

Put my strategies into action. Adopt the Train the Trainer mindset. Start involving your leaders in training events. Start leading training events. Start Coaching Three to Coach Three. Start applying the distinction between what is duplicable and what isn't.

Duplicate taking action on these strategies. Pick one strategy to put into action first. When you've successfully integrated that into the way you and your team do your network marketing, implement another strategy. If you implement just one strategy a month, you can put all these strategies into place within a year. If you take action faster, you can get even faster results. You can start duplicating success today. You've got the formula. Now make it work for you.

About the Authors

ERIC LOFHOLM is a master sales trainer who has helped over 10,000 students make more sales. Trained by best-selling sales expert Dr. Donald Moine, Eric has helped generate nearly $500 million in revenue in the last two decades. Eric honed his skills as a sales trainer for Tony Robbins from 1997 to 1999 before founding his own company, Eric Lofholm International. He offers expert training both for corporate sales departments and for individuals who want to improve their sales skills.

JUDY O'HIGGINS is a master network marketing leader who currently leads a team of nearly 6,000 sales representatives in every state of the United States as well as Canada, the United Kingdom, Ireland, Australia, New Zealand, and Singapore. Judy's current rank is #16 out of 165,000 distributors in her company. She has been with her current company since 2005 and has been training in sales under Eric Lofholm since 2007. Judy holds degrees in Sociology and Social Work and has three decades of experience in these fields, enhancing her sales leadership skills.

To Learn More

To get some free training from Eric, go to:

      www.saleschampion.com

To get free information from Judy on how to increase sponsoring success, go to:

      www.judyohiggins.com

Made in the USA
San Bernardino, CA
14 November 2015